The Step by Step Guide to Drawing Animals

Activity Book

Activivbooks for Kids

INSTRUCTIONS FOR DRAWING:

THIS HOW-TO DRAWING BOOK CONSISTS OF IMAGES THAT ARE PLACED ON GRIDS. THERE IS AN EMPTY DRAWING BOX WITH GRIDS THAT WILL SERVE AS YOUR PRACTICE SPACE. TO COPY EACH IMAGE, DRAW PARTS OF THE IMAGE PER GRID AND PUT THEM ON THE BLANK GRIDS. SOUNDS DIFFICULT? NOT REALLY. TRY IT FIRST!

IT'S OKAY IF YOU DON'T COPY THE IMAGE PERFECTLY. AFTER ALL, DRAWING IS ABOUT THE EXPRESSION OF YOUR PERCEPTION AS WELL AS YOUR HAND STRENGTH AND CONTROL.

WHEN YOU'VE COPIED THE IMAGE, GO AHEAD AND COLOR IT NEXT! WE'RE EXCITED TO SEE WHAT YOU CAN DO!

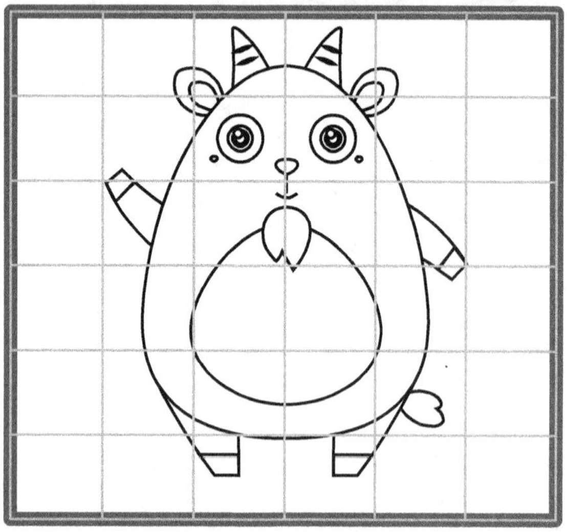

DRAW
THE
IMAGE

DRAW
THE
IMAGE

DRAW

THE IMAGE

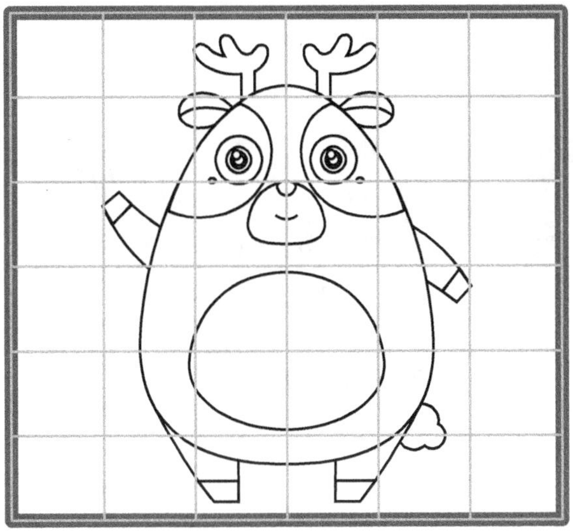

DRAW THE IMAGE

DRAW THE IMAGE

DRAW
THE IMAGE

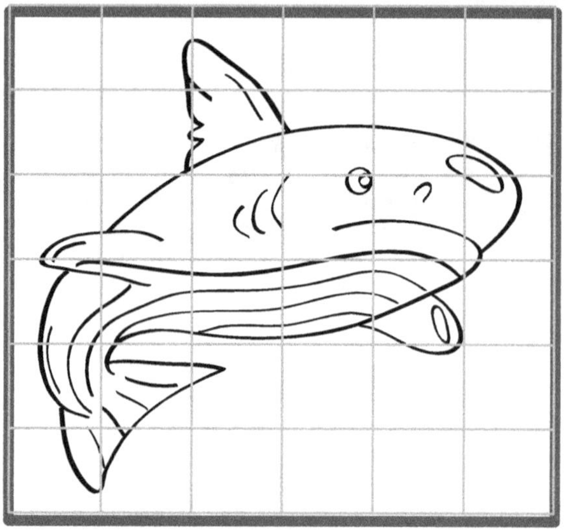

DRAW THE IMAGE

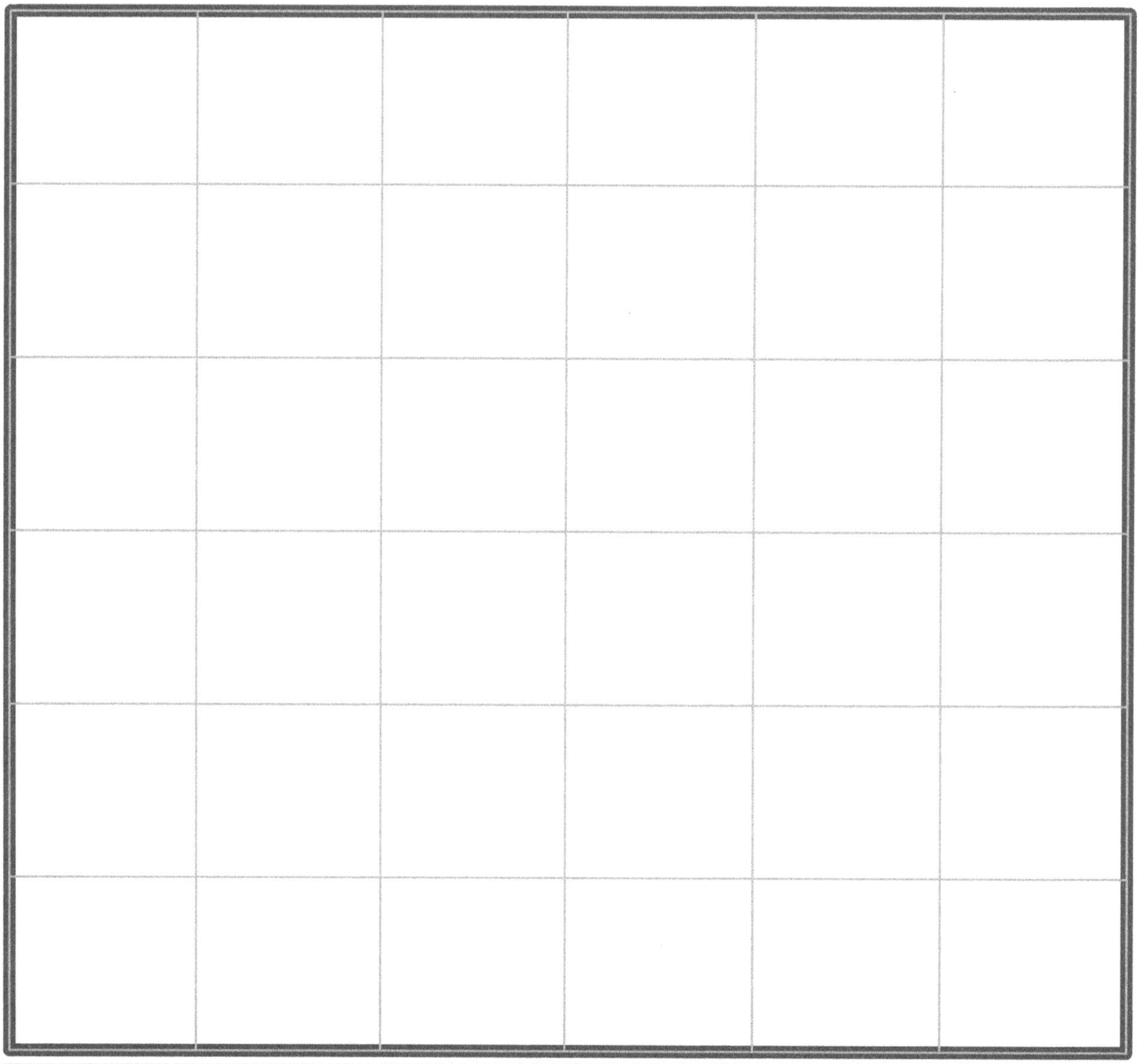

DRAW
THE IMAGE

DRAW THE IMAGE

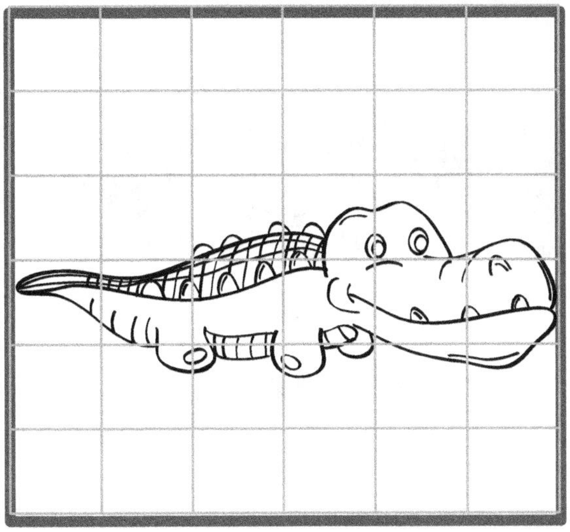

DRAW
THE IMAGE

DRAW
THE IMAGE

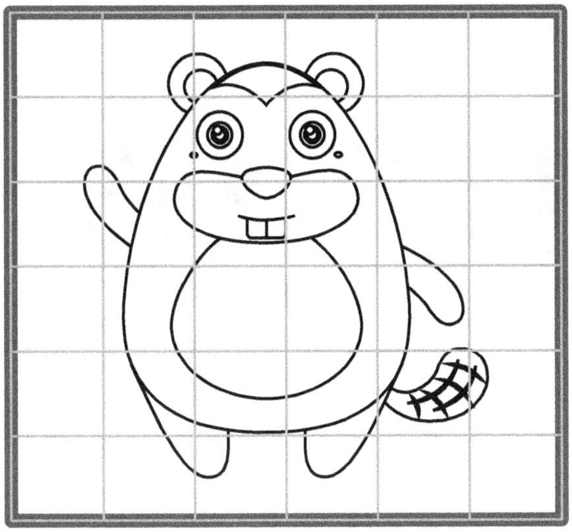

DRAW
THE IMAGE

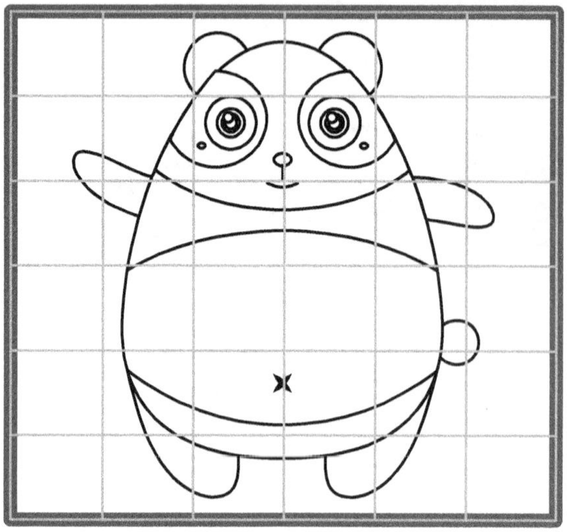

DRAW THE IMAGE

DRAW THE IMAGE

DRAW THE IMAGE

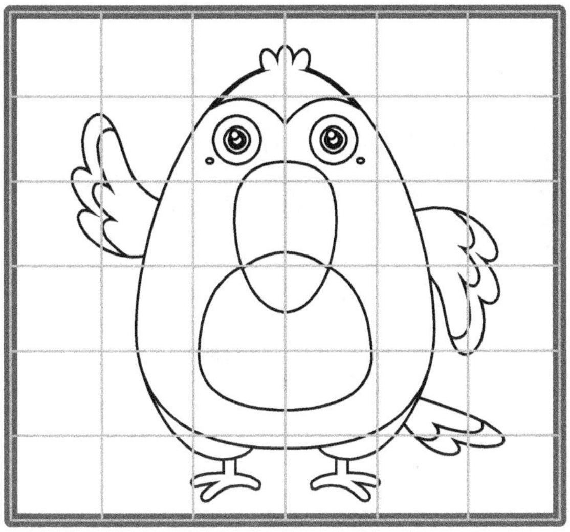

DRAW
THE IMAGE

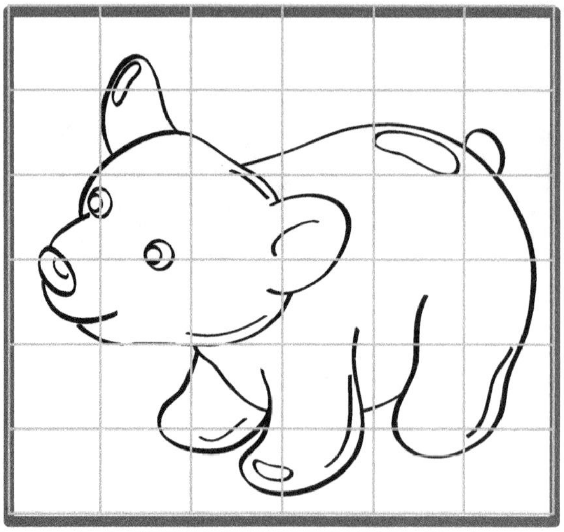

DRAW
THE
IMAGE

DRAW THE IMAGE

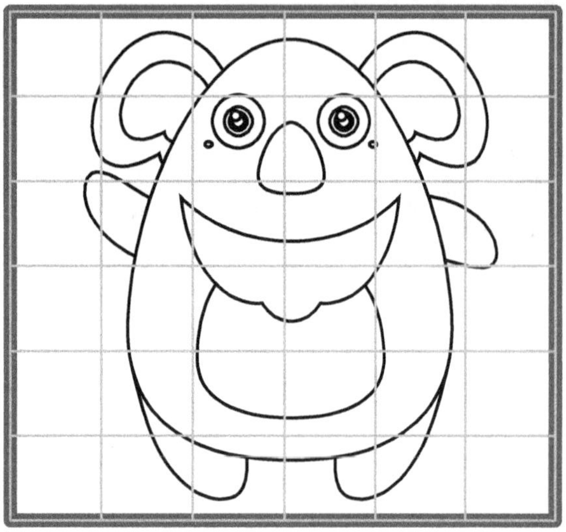

DRAW THE IMAGE

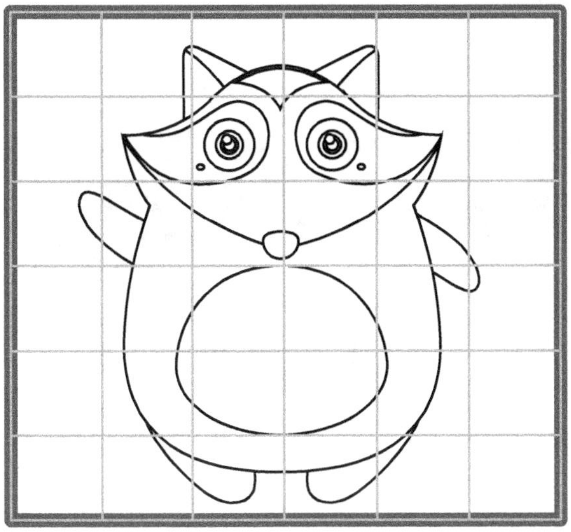

DRAW

THE IMAGE

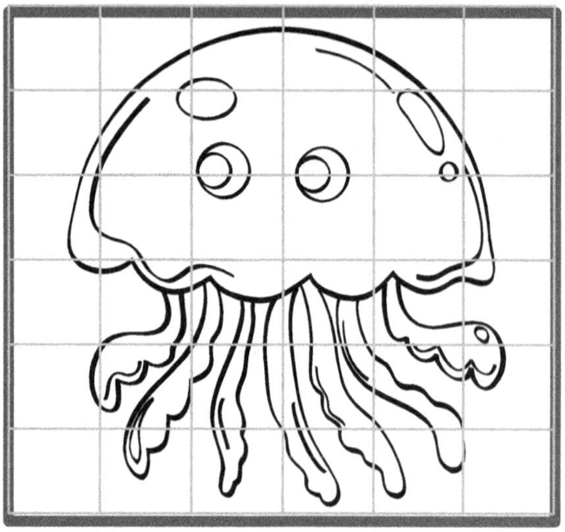

DRAW THE IMAGE

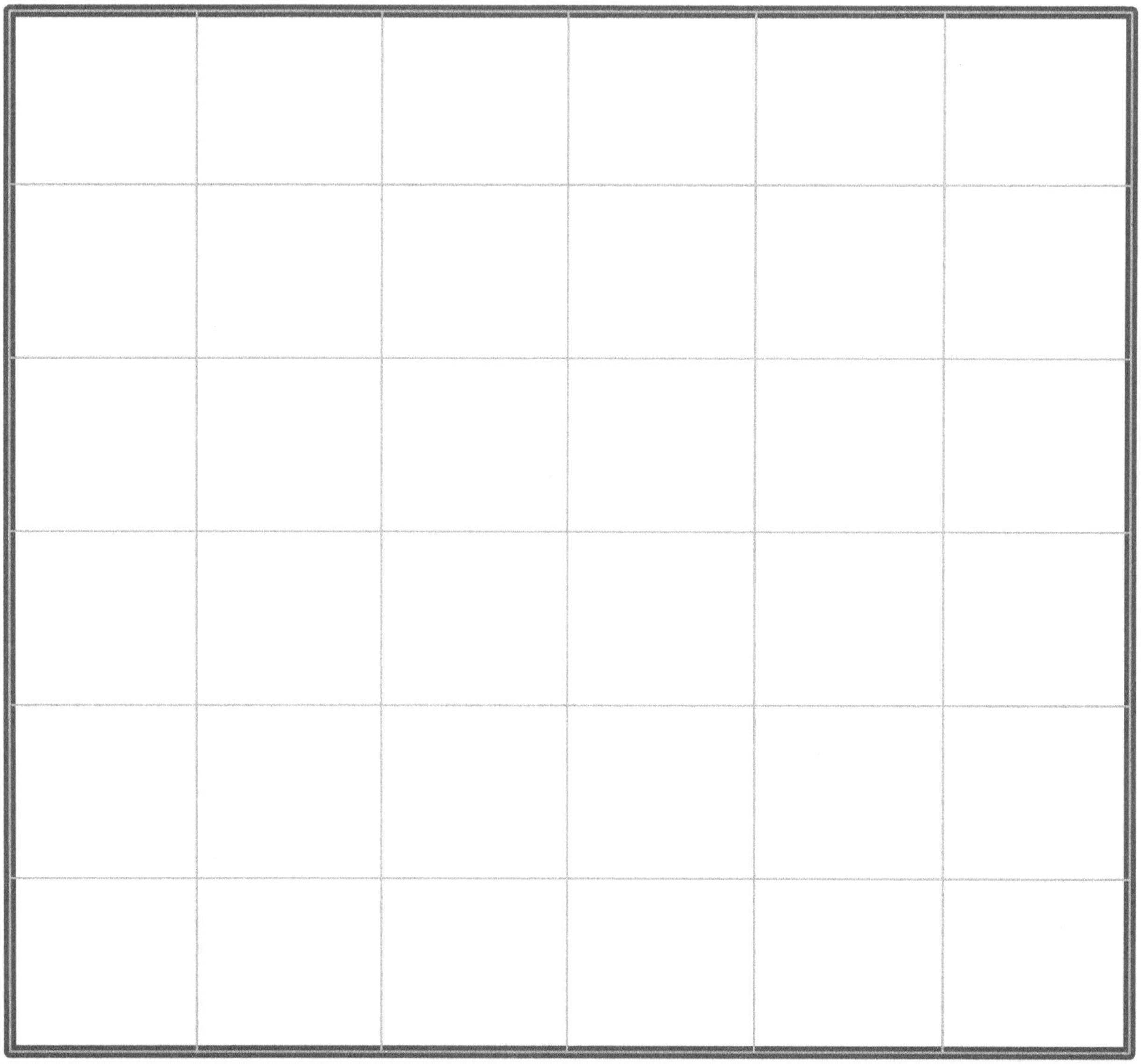

DRAW
THE IMAGE

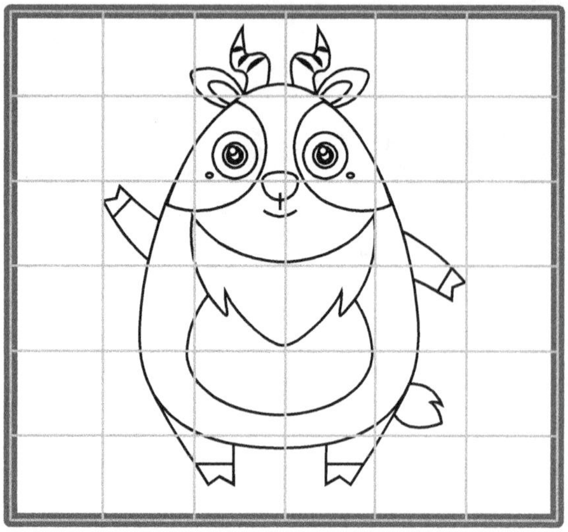

DRAW THE IMAGE

DRAW THE IMAGE

DRAW
THE IMAGE

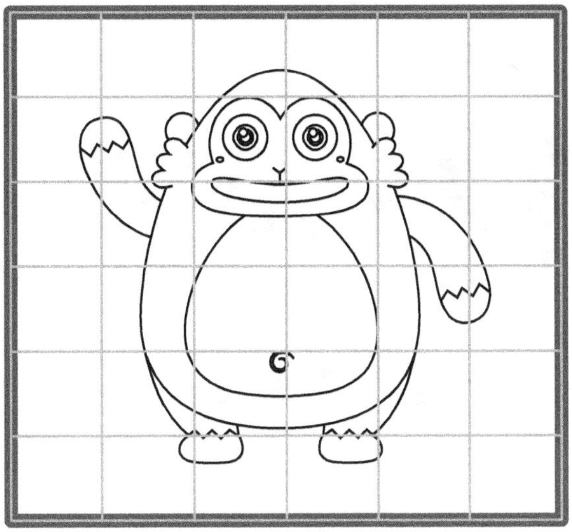

DRAW
THE IMAGE

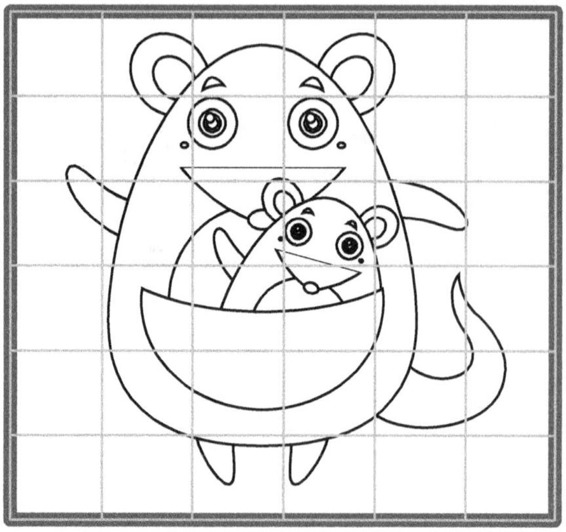

DRAW
THE IMAGE

DRAW THE IMAGE

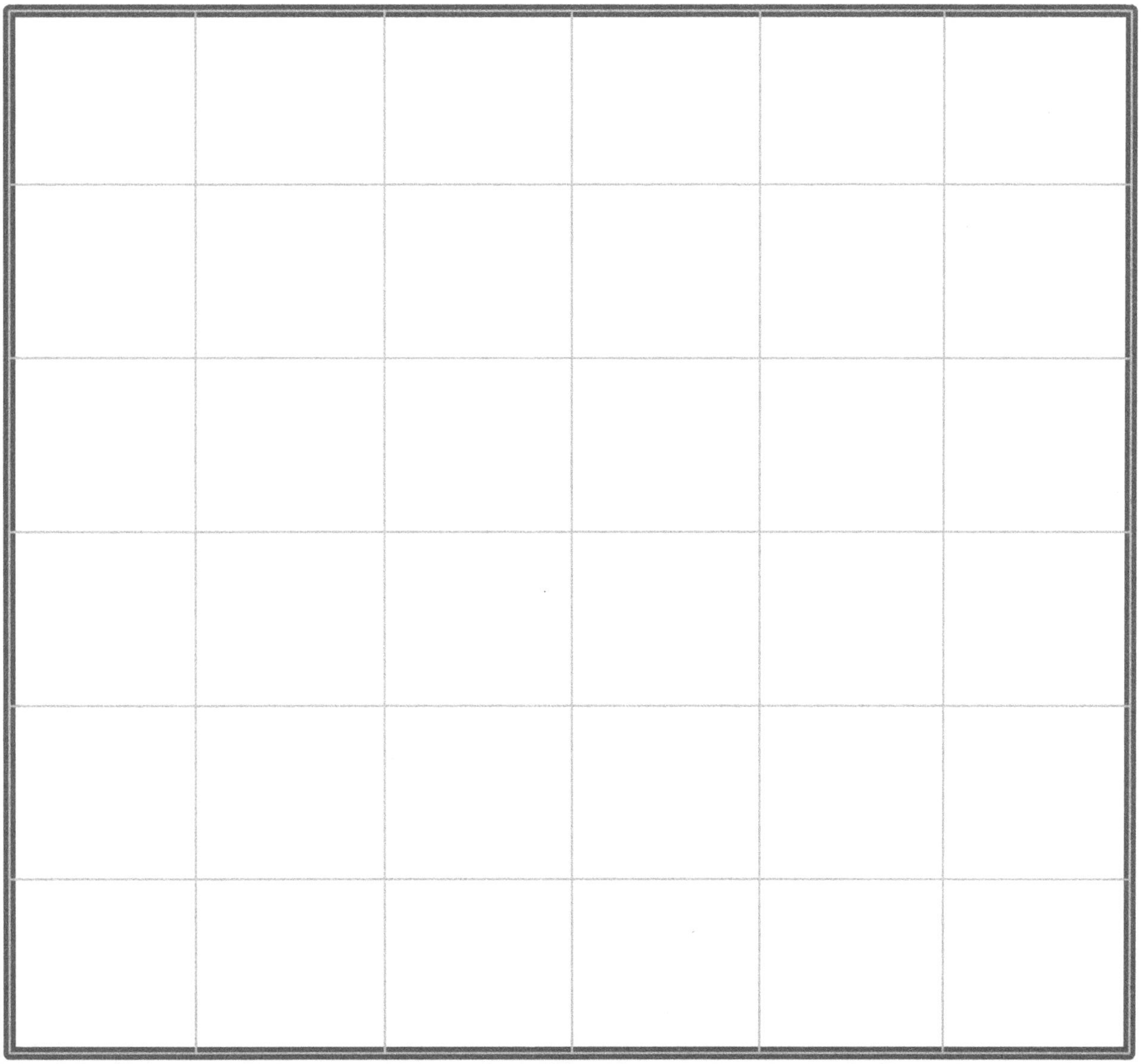

DRAW THE IMAGE

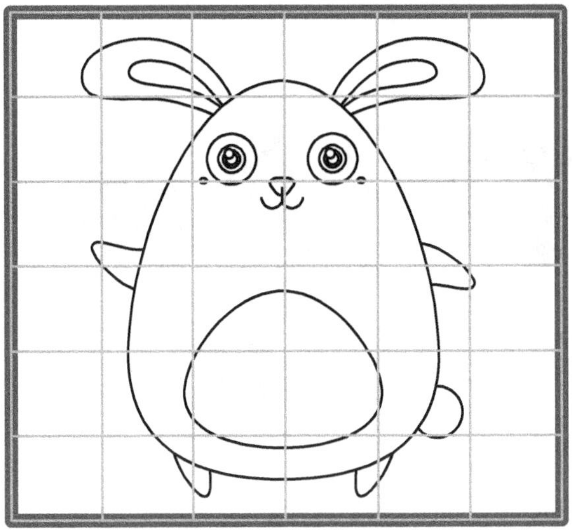

DRAW
THE
IMAGE

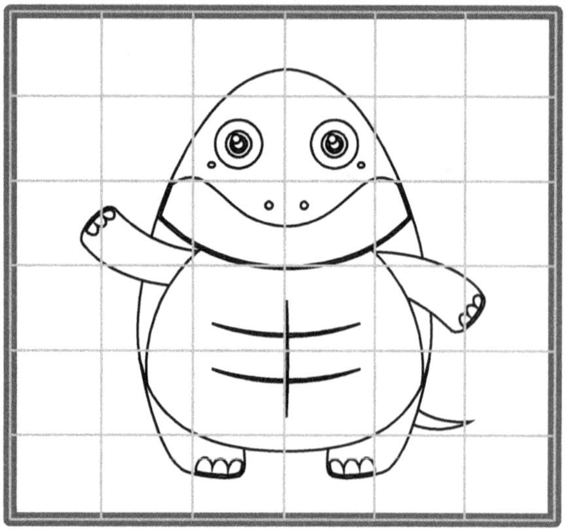

DRAW THE IMAGE

DRAW THE IMAGE

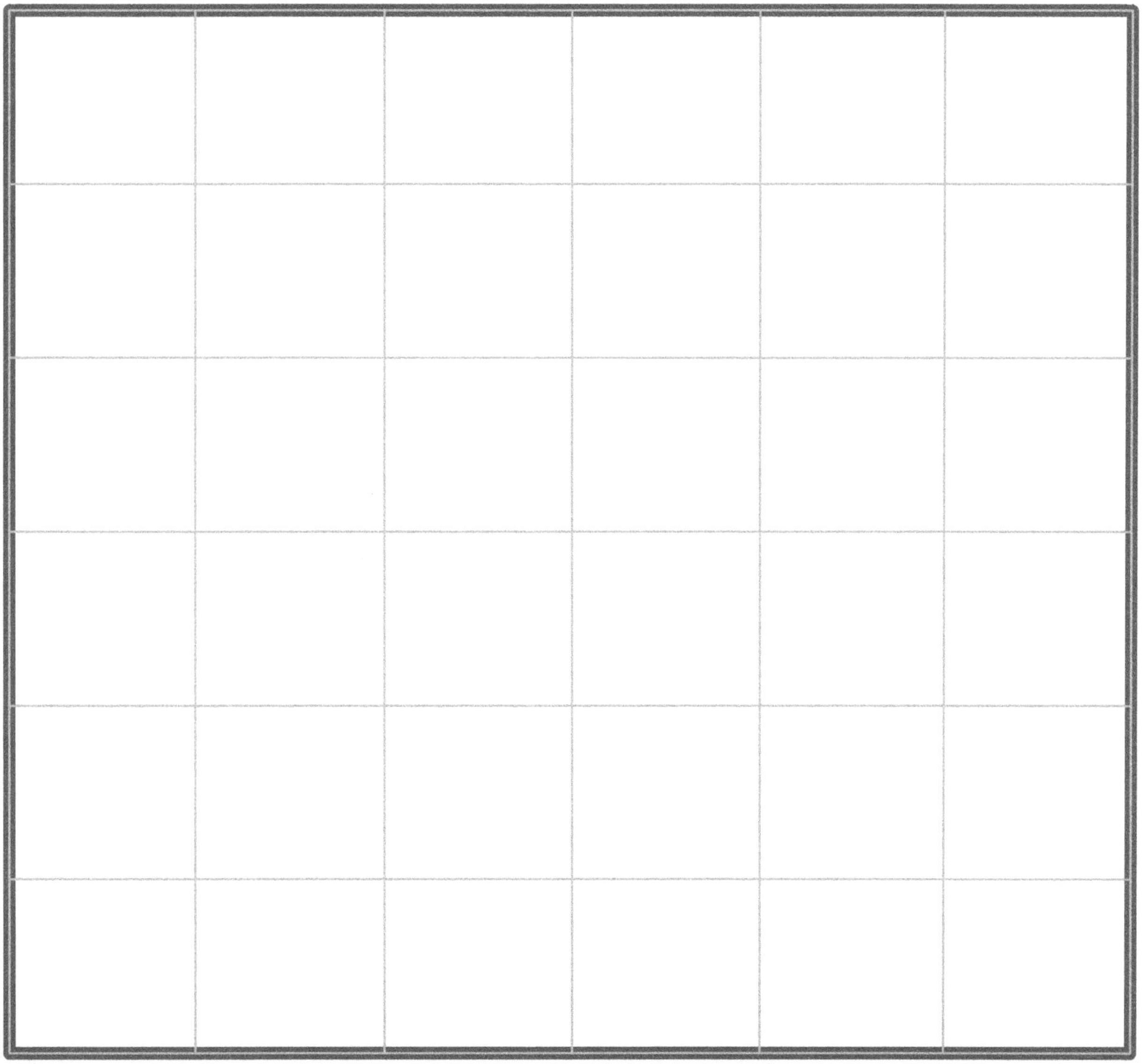

DRAW
THE
IMAGE

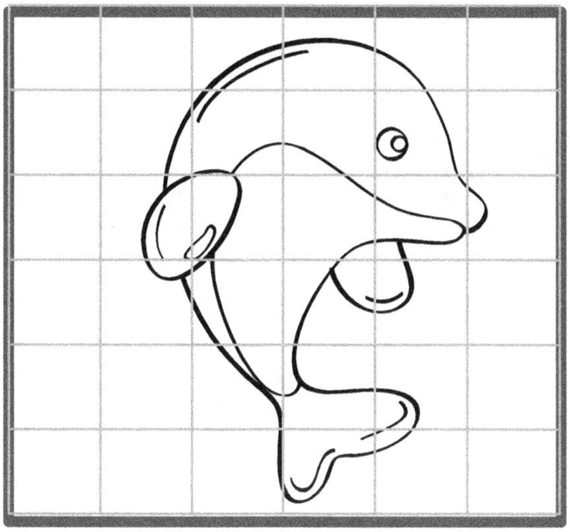

DRAW
THE IMAGE

DRAW THE IMAGE

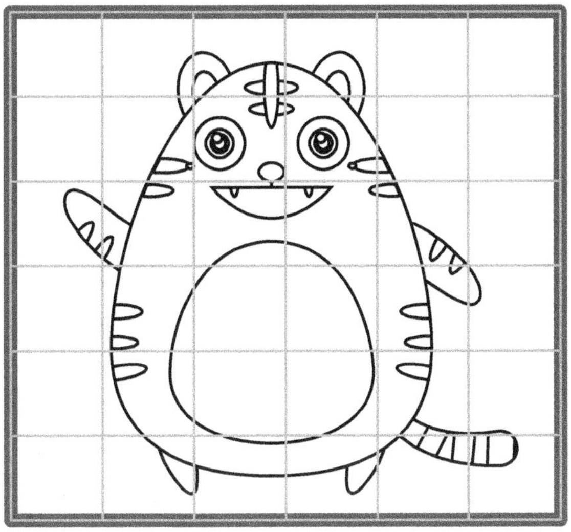

DRAW THE IMAGE

www.ingramcontent.com/pod-product-compliance
Lightning Source LLC
LaVergne TN
LVHW082323080426
835508LV00042B/1525
9781683214458